Pineapple Recipes

Homemade Pineapple Recipe Book for a Healthy Living

Pineapple Wonders Book 4

By Brendan Fawn

Copyright © 2019 Brendan Fawn

All rights reserved.

ISBN: 9781080279562

Text Copyright © [Brendan Fawn]
All rights reserved. No part of this guide may be reproduced in any form without permission in writing from the publisher except in the case of brief quotations embodied in critical articles or reviews.

Legal & Disclaimer
The information contained in this book and its contents is not designed to replace or take the place of any form of medical or professional advice; and is not meant to replace the need for independent medical, financial, legal or other professional advice or services, as may be required. The content and information in this book has been provided for educational and entertainment purposes only.

The content and information contained in this book has been compiled from sources deemed reliable, and it is accurate to the best of the Author's knowledge, information, and belief. However, the Author cannot guarantee its accuracy and validity and cannot be held liable for any errors and/or omissions. Further, changes are periodically made to this book as and when needed. Where appropriate and/or necessary, you must consult a professional (including but not limited to your doctor, attorney, financial advisor or such other professional advisor) before using any of the suggested remedies, techniques, or information in this book.

Upon using the contents and information contained in this book, you agree to hold harmless the Author from and against any damages, costs, and expenses, including any legal fees potentially resulting from the application of any of the information provided by this book. This disclaimer applies to any loss, damages or injury caused by the use and application, whether directly or indirectly, of any advice or information presented, whether for breach of contract, tort, negligence, personal injury, criminal intent, or under any other cause of action.

You agree to accept all risks of using the information presented in this book.

You agree that by continuing to read this book, where appropriate and/or necessary, you shall consult a professional (including but not limited to your doctor, attorney, or financial advisor or such other advisor as needed) before using any of the suggested remedies, techniques, or information in this book.

Introduction 7

Chapter I: Hot Dishes 8

Pineapple with Chicken and Eggplant 8

Pineapple with Chicken and Squash 10

Pineapple with Chicken and Sweetcorns 12

Pineapple, Pumpkin and Pork 14

Pineapple, Pumpkin and Pork in the White Wine 16

Pineapple, Beer and Pork 18

Pork in Mayonnaise and Pineapples 20

Beef in Mayonnaise and Pineapples 22

Lamb with Pineapples 24

Pineapple with Beef and Onions 26

Chapter II: Pineapple Soups 28

Pineapple Soup with Cabbage 28

Pineapple Soup with Squash 30

Pineapple Soup with Pumpkin 32

Sour Pineapple Soup 34

Pineapple Soup with Bananas and Peanuts 36

Pineapple Soup with Peaches and Peanuts 38

Pineapple Soup with Strawberries and Peanuts 40

Pineapple and Coconut Soup with Cherries 42

Pineapple and Coconut Soup with Strawberries 44

Pineapple and Coconut Soup with Blueberries 46

Chapter III: Pineapple Salads 48

Pineapple and Melon Salad with Strawberries 48

Pineapple and Melon Salad with Kiwis 50

Pineapple and Melon Salad with Pears 52

Pineapple Salad with Melon and Apples 54

Pineapple Salad with Melon and Plums 56

Pineapple Salad with Melon and Hazelnuts 58

Pineapple, Raspberry and Honey Salad 61

Pineapple, Strawberry and Honey Salad 62

Pineapple, Blueberry and Honey Salad 64

Pineapple, Oats and Honey Salad 66

Pineapple Salad with Pears and Cottage Cheese 68

Pineapple Salad with Peaches and Cottage Cheese 70

Pineapple Salad with Apricots and Cottage Cheese 72

Pineapple Salad with Bananas and Cottage Cheese 74

Pineapple Salad with Strawberries, Cottage Cheese and Cashews 76

Pineapple, Oats and Apples Salad 78

Pineapple, Oats and Oranges Salad 80

Pineapple, Oats and Cherry Salad 82

Spiralized Pineapple Salad with Cranberries and Hazelnuts 84

Spiralized Pineapple Salad with Peach Jam 86

Spiralized Pineapple Salad with Strawberry Jam 88

Pineapple and Blueberries Salad with Mango and Raspberries 90

Pineapple and Blueberries Salad with Kiwis and Raspberries 92

Pineapple Salad with Sour Cream and Berries 94

Pineapple Salad with Sour Cream and Kiwis 96

Pineapple Salad with Sour Cream and Bananas 98

Chapter IV: Pineapple Pies 100

Pineapple Pie with Strawberries 100

Pineapple Pie with Raspberries 102

Pineapple Pie with Blueberries 104

Pineapple Pie with Gooseberries 106

Pineapple Pie with Apples, Cinnamon and Hazelnuts 108

Pineapple Pie with Cottage Cheese 110

Pineapple Pie with Apples and Honey 113

Conclusion 115

Recipe Index 116

Introduction

This pineapple recipe book was created to help you prepare tasty pineapple recipes. Anyone who wants to try new tastes can benefit from this pineapple cookbook.

This book has various pineapple recipes, such as sweet pineapple desserts, pineapple salads, soups or hot dishes. You should use your imagination because there is no limit to what you can cook when using pineapple as the main ingredient. This pineapple recipe cookbook was created to inspire you to discover a colorful world of exotic pineapple cooking!

What is more, you don't need to be a professional 28 Michelin Star chef to use pineapple recipes from this cookbook and to prepare pineapple food for yourself or your family. I would like to encourage you to test new pineapple recipes and experiment by adding your own flavors!

Chapter I: Hot Dishes

Pineapple with Chicken and Eggplant

Prep Time: 15 min. | Cooking Time: 60 min. | Servings: 5

Ingredients:

1 fresh pineapple, peeled and cubed

20 oz chicken, cubed

4 medium eggplants, peeled and cubed

1 cayenne pepper

1 onion, peeled and chopped

7 garlic cloves, chopped

2 tablespoons garlic powder

5 tablespoons of Olive oil

4 teaspoons lemon juice

salt and pepper

basil

How to Prepare:

1. Marinate the chicken meat overnight in the cubed pineapple, cayenne pepper, chopped garlic, garlic powder and onion. Add in some lemon juice.
2. Preheat the oven to 290°-320° Fahrenheit and bake the pineapple and chicken with the eggplants, oil, garlic powder, garlic, onion, salt, pepper and basil for 50-60 minutes until the chicken meat is soft.
3. Pour the lemon juice over the baked pineapple, chicken and eggplants and serve with the white wine.

Nutritional Information:

Calories: 302; Total fat: 34 oz; Total carbohydrates: 49 oz; Protein: 24 oz

Pineapple with Chicken and Squash

Prep Time: 25 min. | Cooking Time: 60 min. | Servings: 5

Ingredients:

1 fresh pineapple, peeled and cubed

20 oz chicken breast, cubed

2 squashes, peeled and cubed

1 cayenne pepper

1 onion, peeled and chopped

7 garlic cloves, chopped

2 tablespoons garlic powder

5 tablespoons of Olive oil

4 teaspoons lemon juice

salt and pepper

basil

How to Prepare:

1. Marinate the chicken meat overnight in the cubed pineapple, cayenne pepper, chopped garlic, garlic powder and onion. Add in some lemon juice.
2. Preheat the oven to 290°-320° Fahrenheit and bake the pineapple and chicken with the squashes, oil, garlic powder, garlic, onion, salt, pepper and basil for 50-60 minutes until the chicken meat is soft.
3. Pour the lemon juice over the baked pineapple, chicken and squashes and serve with the white wine.

Nutritional Information:

Calories: 301; Total fat: 33 oz; Total carbohydrates: 46 oz; Protein: 22 oz

Pineapple with Chicken and Sweetcorns

Prep Time: 15 min. | Cooking Time: 60 min. | Servings: 5

Ingredients:

1 fresh pineapple, peeled and cubed

20 oz chicken, cubed

4 cups of fresh sweetcorns

1 cayenne pepper

1 onion, peeled and chopped

7 garlic cloves, chopped

2 tablespoons garlic powder

5 tablespoons of Olive oil

4 teaspoons lemon juice

salt and pepper

basil

How to Prepare:

1. Marinate the chicken meat overnight in the cubed pineapple, cayenne pepper, chopped garlic, garlic powder and onion. Add in some lemon juice.

2. Preheat the oven to 290°-320° Fahrenheit and bake the pineapple and chicken with the sweetcorns, oil, garlic powder, garlic, onion, salt, pepper and basil for 45-50 minutes until the chicken meat is soft.
3. Pour the lemon juice over the baked pineapple, chicken and sweetcorns and serve with the white wine.

Nutritional Information:

Calories: 304; Total fat: 35 oz; Total carbohydrates: 50 oz; Protein: 25 oz

Pineapple, Pumpkin and Pork

Prep Time: 20 min. | Cooking Time: 80 min. | Servings: 4

Ingredients:

5 cups of fresh pineapple, peeled and cubed

20 oz pork, cubed

3 cups of pumpkin, peeled and cubed

6 potatoes, peeled and cubed

1 chili pepper

1 red onion, peeled and chopped

10 cloves of garlic, chopped

4 tablespoons garlic powder

1 cup of olive oil

4 teaspoons lemon juice

salt and pepper

nutmeg

How to Prepare:

1. Marinate the cubed pork meat overnight in the cubed pineapple, chili pepper, chopped garlic and onion. Add in some lemon juice.
2. Heat the wok or frying pan and stew the pork cubes for 10-20 minutes with the closed lid.
3. Preheat the oven to 270°-290° Fahrenheit and bake the pineapple and pork with the pumpkin, potatoes, oil, garlic powder, garlic, onion, salt, pepper and nutmeg for around 45-60 minutes until the meat is soft.
4. Pour the lemon juice over the baked pineapple, pork and pumpkin cubes and then serve.

Nutritional Information:

Calories: 318; Total fat: 32 oz; Total carbohydrates: 47 oz; Protein: 24 oz

Pineapple, Pumpkin and Pork in the White Wine

Prep Time: 20 min. | Cooking Time: 80 min. | Servings: 4

Ingredients:

5 cups of fresh pineapple, peeled and cubed

25 oz pork, cubed

2 glasses of white wine

3 cups of pumpkin, peeled and cubed

5 potatoes, peeled and cubed

1 chili pepper

1 red onion, peeled and chopped

10 cloves of garlic, chopped

4 tablespoons garlic powder

1 cup of olive oil

4 teaspoons lemon juice

salt and pepper

nutmeg

How to Prepare:

1. Marinate the cubed pork meat overnight in the white wine.

2. Heat the wok or frying pan and stew the pork cubes for 10-20 minutes with the closed lid.
3. Preheat the oven to 270°-290° Fahrenheit and bake the pineapple and pork with the pumpkin, potatoes, oil, garlic powder, garlic, onion, salt, pepper and nutmeg for around 45-60 minutes until the meat is soft.
4. Pour the lemon juice over the baked pineapple, pork and pumpkin cubes and then serve.

Nutritional Information:

Calories: 317; Total fat: 31 oz; Total carbohydrates: 46 oz; Protein: 26 oz

Pineapple, Beer and Pork

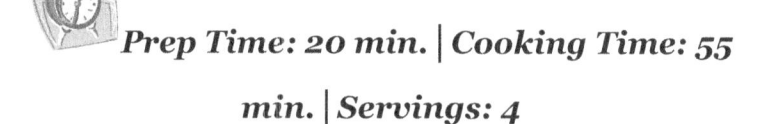

Prep Time: 20 min. | Cooking Time: 55 min. | Servings: 4

Ingredients:

5 cups of fresh pineapple, peeled and cubed

2-3 cups of dark beer (Lager or Munich Dunkel)

25 oz pork, cubed

1 cup of pumpkin, peeled and cubed

5 potatoes, peeled and cubed

1 chili pepper

1 onion, peeled and chopped

10 cloves of garlic, chopped

4 tablespoons garlic powder

1 cup of olive oil

4 teaspoons lemon juice

salt and pepper

nutmeg

How to Prepare:

1. Marinate the cubed pork meat overnight in the dark beer.

2. Heat the wok or frying pan and stew the pork cubes for 10-20 minutes with the closed lid.
3. Preheat the oven to 270°-290° Fahrenheit and bake the pineapple and pork with the pumpkin, potatoes, oil, garlic powder, garlic, onion, salt, pepper and nutmeg for around 45-60 minutes until the meat is soft.
4. Pour the lemon juice over the baked pineapple, pork and pumpkin cubes and then serve.

Nutritional Information:

Calories: 327; Total fat: 39 oz; Total carbohydrates: 52 oz; Protein: 34 oz

Pork in Mayonnaise and Pineapples

Prep Time: 20 min. | Cooking Time: 40-50 min. | Servings: 5

Ingredients:

4 cups of fresh pineapple, peeled and cubed

20 oz pork, cubed

4 cups of mayonnaise

2 onions, peeled and chopped

4 tomatoes, cubed

6 tablespoons Olive oil

4 tablespoons soy sauce

4 tablespoons freshly squeezed lemon juice

2 tablespoons powdered garlic

salt and pepper

How to Prepare:

1. In a bowl, combine the powdered garlic, pepper and some salt. Season the cubed pork with the salt, pepper and powdered garlic mix. Combine the mayonnaise and cubed pineapples with the meat and marinate the pork meat overnight.
2. Heat the oil in a skillet and stew the cubed pork meat with the closed lid for around 30-40 minutes. Few minutes before the pork meat is ready mix in the chopped onions, and stew the pork cubes for a further 10 minutes. Combine the soy sauce with the cubed tomatoes and spoon over the pork.
3. Sprinkle the salt and pepper and pour the freshly squeezed lemon juice over the pork and you are free to serve the pork meat in separate dishes. Remember that this dish should be served warm.

Nutritional Information:

Calories: 349; Total fat: 59 oz; Total carbohydrates: 75 oz; Protein: 37 oz

Beef in Mayonnaise and Pineapples

Prep Time: 20 min. | Cooking Time: 40-50 min. | Servings: 5

Ingredients:

5 cups of fresh pineapple, peeled and cubed

25 oz beef, cubed

5 cups of mayonnaise

2 onions, peeled and chopped

4 tomatoes, cubed

6 tablespoons Olive oil

4 tablespoons soy sauce

4 tablespoons freshly squeezed lemon juice

2 tablespoons powdered garlic

salt and pepper

How to Prepare:

1. In a bowl, combine the powdered garlic, pepper and some salt. Season the cubed beef with the salt, pepper and powdered garlic mix. Combine the mayonnaise and cubed pineapples with the meat and marinate the beef meat overnight.

2. Heat the oil in a skillet and stew the cubed beef meat with the closed lid for around 30-40 minutes. Few minutes before the beef meat is ready mix in the chopped onions, and stew the beef cubes for a further 10 minutes. Combine the soy sauce with the cubed tomatoes and spoon over the beef.

3. Sprinkle the salt and pepper and pour the freshly squeezed lemon juice over the beef and you are free to serve the beef meat in separate dishes. Remember that this dish should be served warm.

Nutritional Information:

Calories: 345; Total fat: 56 oz; Total carbohydrates: 72 oz; Protein: 36 oz

Lamb with Pineapples

Prep Time: 25 min. | Cooking Time: 60 min. | Servings: 4

Ingredients:

5 cups of fresh pineapple, peeled and cubed

1 cup of pineapple juice

25 oz lamb, cubed

2 onions, peeled and chopped

4 tomatoes, cubed

6 tablespoons Olive oil

4 tablespoons soy sauce

4 tablespoons freshly squeezed lemon juice

2 tablespoons powdered garlic

salt and pepper

How to Prepare:

1. In a bowl, combine the powdered garlic, pepper and some salt. Season the cubed lamb with the salt, pepper and powdered garlic mix. Combine the pineapple juice and the cubed pineapples with the meat and marinate the lamb meat overnight.

2. Heat the oil in a skillet and stew the cubed lamb meat with the closed lid for around 40-50 minutes. Few minutes before the lamb meat is ready mix in the chopped onions, and stew the lamb cubes for a further 10 minutes. Combine the soy sauce with the cubed tomatoes and spoon over the lamb.

3. Sprinkle the salt and pepper and pour the freshly squeezed lemon juice over the lamb and you are free to serve the lamb meat in separate dishes. Remember that this dish should be served warm.

Nutritional Information:

Calories: 375; Total fat: 64 oz; Total carbohydrates: 78 oz; Protein: 46 oz

Pineapple with Beef and Onions

Prep Time: 20 min. | Cooking Time: 80 min. | Servings: 4

Ingredients:

5 cups of fresh pineapple, peeled and cubed

4 cups of onions, chopped

25 oz beef, cubed

5 potatoes, peeled and cubed

2 tomatoes, cubed

1 chili pepper

10 cloves of garlic, chopped

4 tablespoons garlic powder

1 cup of olive oil

3 tablespoons lemon juice

salt and pepper

nutmeg

How to Prepare:

1. Marinate the chopped beef meat overnight in the onions, salt and pepper.
2. Heat the wok or frying pan and stew the beef cubes for 10-20 minutes with the closed lid.
3. Preheat the oven to 270°-290° Fahrenheit and bake the pineapple and beef with the potatoes, garlic powder, garlic, onion, tomatoes, salt, pepper and nutmeg for around 45-60 minutes until the meat is soft.
4. Pour the lemon juice over the baked pineapple, beef and onions and then serve.

Nutritional Information:

Calories: 337; Total fat: 40 oz; Total carbohydrates: 50 oz; Protein: 32 oz

Chapter II: Pineapple Soups

Pineapple Soup with Cabbage

Prep Time: 15 min. | Cooking Time: 40 min. | Servings: 4

Ingredients:

1 cup of pineapples, canned

1 cabbage, chopped

2 carrots, grated

4 potatoes, cubed

2 onions, chopped

2 tablespoons Olive oil

5 cups of water

1 cup of white flour

1 teaspoon citric acid

salt and pepper

How to Cook:

1. Peel and cut the pineapple into small cubes or use canned pineapple.

2. In a pan, boil the pineapple with the carrots, potatoes, onions and cabbage for around 10-15 minutes until the pineapple and vegetables are soft.
3. Mash the pineapple and vegetables using a blender, food processor or potato masher until the creamy consistency and homogenous mass.
4. Boil the water and cook the noodles for 15 minutes or follow the cooking time suggested on the packet.
5. In a saucepan, combine the water with all the ingredients and then cook for 10-15 minutes to serve warm.

Nutritional Information:

Calories: 117; Total fat: 11 oz; Total carbohydrates: 20 oz; Protein: 9 oz

Pineapple Soup with Squash

Prep Time: 15 min. | Cooking Time: 40 min. | Servings: 4

Ingredients:

1 cup of pineapples, canned

1 squash, chopped

2 carrots, grated

4 potatoes, cubed

2 onions, chopped

2 tablespoons Olive oil

5 cups of water

1 cup of white flour

1 teaspoon citric acid

salt and pepper

How to Cook:

1. Peel and cut the pineapple into small cubes or use canned pineapple.
2. In a pan, boil the pineapple with the carrots, potatoes, onions and squash for around 10-15 minutes until the pineapple and vegetables are soft.
3. Mash the pineapple and vegetables using a blender, food processor or potato masher until they have a creamy consistency and homogenous mass.
4. Boil the water and cook the noodles for 15 minutes or follow the cooking time suggested on the packet.
5. In a saucepan, combine the water with all the ingredients and then cook for 10-15 minutes to serve warm with the cream.

Nutritional Information:

Calories: 124; Total fat: 14 oz; Total carbohydrates: 22 oz; Protein: 11 oz

Pineapple Soup with Pumpkin

Prep Time: 15 min. | Cooking Time: 40 min. | Servings: 4

Ingredients:

1 cup of pineapples, canned

1 small pumpkin, chopped

2 carrots, grated

4 potatoes, cubed

2 onions, chopped

2 tablespoons Olive oil

5 cups of water

1 cup of white flour

1 teaspoon citric acid

salt and pepper

How to Cook:

1. Peel and cut the pineapple into small cubes or use canned pineapple.

2. In a pan, boil the pineapple with the carrots, potatoes, onions and pumpkin for around 10-15 minutes until the pineapple and vegetables are soft.
3. Mash the pineapple and vegetables using a blender, food processor or potato masher until they have a creamy consistency and homogenous mass.
4. Boil the water and cook the noodles for 15 minutes or follow the cooking time suggested on the packet.
5. In a saucepan, combine the water with all the ingredients and then cook for 10-15 minutes to serve warm with the cream.

Nutritional Information:

Calories: 127; Total fat: 16 oz; Total carbohydrates: 27 oz; Protein: 13 oz

Sour Pineapple Soup

Prep Time: 15 min. | Cooking Time: 40 min. | Servings: 4

Ingredients:

1 cup of pineapples, canned

2 carrots, grated

4 potatoes, cubed

2 onions, chopped

4 tablespoons lemon juice

5 cups of water

1 cup of white flour

salt and pepper

How to Cook:

1. Peel and cut the pineapple into small cubes or use canned pineapple.
2. In a pan, boil the pineapple with the carrots, potatoes and onions for around 10-15 minutes until the pineapple and vegetables are soft.
3. Mash the pineapple and vegetables using a blender, food processor or potato masher until they have a creamy consistency and homogenous mass.
4. Boil the water and cook the noodles for 15 minutes or follow the cooking time suggested on the packet.
5. In a saucepan, combine the water with all the ingredients and then cook for 10-15 minutes to serve warm with the cream.

Nutritional Information:

Calories: 125; Total fat: 15 oz; Total carbohydrates: 25 oz; Protein: 12 oz

Pineapple Soup with Bananas and Peanuts

Prep Time: 5 min. | Cooking Time: 40 min. | Servings: 2

Ingredients:

1 fresh pineapple

2 bananas, peeled and cubed

2 cups of peanuts

5 tablespoons coconut oil

1 cup of white flour

5 tablespoons brown sugar

1 cup of oat milk

spray cream

How to Cook:

1. Peel and cut the pineapple into small cubes or use canned pineapples.
2. Preheat the oven to 250°- 270° Fahrenheit and roast the peanuts in the oven for 10 minutes until lightly browned and crispy, then set aside to cool completely. Grind the peanuts using a food processor or blender.
3. In a pan, boil the pineapple for around 10-15 minutes until the pineapple is soft.
4. Mash the pineapple and bananas using a blender, food processor or potato masher until they have a creamy consistency and homogenous mass.
5. In a saucepan, combine the pineapple-bananas mixture, coconut oil, oat milk, peanuts, white flour and sugar, and then cook for around 10 minutes to serve warm with the spray cream on top.

Nutritional Information:

Calories: 121; Total fat: 14 oz; Total carbohydrates: 24 oz; Protein: 12 oz

Pineapple Soup with Peaches and Peanuts

Prep Time: 10 min. | Cooking Time: 40 min. | Servings: 2

Ingredients:

1 fresh pineapple

5 peaches pitted and cubed

2 cups of peanuts

5 tablespoons coconut oil

1 cup of white flour

5 tablespoons brown sugar

1 cup of oat milk

spray cream

How to Cook:

1. Peel and cut the pineapple into small cubes or use canned pineapples.
2. Preheat the oven to 250°- 270° Fahrenheit and roast the peanuts in the oven for 10 minutes until lightly browned and crispy, then set aside to cool completely. Grind the peanuts using a food processor or blender.

3. In a pan, boil the pineapple for around 10-15 minutes until the pineapple is soft.
4. Mash the pineapple and peaches using a blender, food processor or potato masher until they have a creamy consistency and homogenous mass.
5. In a saucepan, combine the pineapple-peaches mixture, coconut oil, oat milk, peanuts, white flour and sugar, and then cook for around 10 minutes to serve warm with the spray cream on top.

Nutritional Information:

Calories: 123; Total fat: 15 oz; Total carbohydrates: 26 oz; Protein: 13 oz

Pineapple Soup with Strawberries and Peanuts

Prep Time: 5 min. | Cooking Time: 40 min. | Servings: 2

Ingredients:

1 fresh pineapple

4 cups of strawberries

2 cups of peanuts

5 tablespoons coconut oil

1 cup of white flour

5 tablespoons sugar

1 cup of milk

spray cream

How to Cook:

1. Peel and cut the pineapple into small cubes or use canned pineapples.
2. Preheat the oven to 250°- 270° Fahrenheit and roast the peanuts in the oven for 10 minutes until lightly browned and crispy, then set aside to cool completely. Grind the peanuts using a food processor or blender.

3. Mash the pineapple and strawberries with the sugar using a blender, food processor or potato masher until they have a creamy consistency and homogenous mass.
4. In a saucepan, combine the pineapple-strawberries mixture, coconut oil, milk, peanuts and white flour, and then cook for around 10 minutes to serve warm with the spray cream on top.

<u>Nutritional Information:</u>

Calories: 129; Total fat: 24 oz; Total carbohydrates: 44 oz; Protein: 19 oz

Pineapple and Coconut Soup with Cherries

Prep Time: 15 min. | Cooking Time: 45 min. | Servings: 4

Ingredients:

1 fresh pineapple, peeled and cubed

1 cup of coconut milk

5 tablespoons coconut oil

2 cups of fresh cherries, pitted

1 cup of cherry jam

4 tablespoons sugar

How to Cook:

1. Combine the pineapple with the cherry jam, cherries, and coconut oil and then mash the fruits using a potato masher or blender until they have a creamy consistency and homogenous mass.
2. In a saucepan, combine the mashed pineapple, cherry jam, cherries, and coconut oil with the sugar. Add the coconut milk and then boil for 10-15 minutes. Serve warm with the fresh cherries.

Nutritional Information:

Calories: 99; Total fat: 18 oz; Total carbohydrates: 26 oz; Protein: 12 oz

Pineapple and Coconut Soup with Strawberries

Prep Time: 15 min. | Cooking Time: 45 min. | Servings: 4

Ingredients:

1 fresh pineapple, peeled and cubed

1 cup of coconut milk

5 tablespoons coconut oil

2 cups of fresh strawberries

1 cup of strawberry jam

5 tablespoons sugar

How to Cook:

1. Combine the pineapple with the strawberry jam, strawberries, and coconut oil and then mash the fruits using a potato masher or blender until they have a creamy consistency and homogenous mass.
2. In a saucepan, combine the mashed pineapple, strawberry jam, strawberries, and coconut oil with the sugar. Add the coconut milk and then boil for 10-15 minutes. Serve warm with the fresh strawberries.

Nutritional Information:

Calories: 109; Total fat: 21 oz; Total carbohydrates: 34 oz; Protein: 16 oz

Pineapple and Coconut Soup with Blueberries

Prep Time: 15 min. | Cooking Time: 45 min. | Servings: 4

Ingredients:

1 fresh pineapple, peeled and cubed

1 cup of coconut milk

5 tablespoons coconut oil

2 cups of fresh blueberries

1 cup of blueberry jam

5 tablespoons sugar

1 tablespoon liquid honey

How to Cook:

1. Combine the pineapple with the blueberry jam, blueberries, honey, and coconut oil and then mash them using a potato masher or blender until they have a creamy consistency and homogenous mass.
2. In a saucepan, combine the mashed pineapple, blueberry jam, blueberries, and coconut oil with the sugar. Add the

coconut milk and then boil for 10-15 minutes. Serve warm with the fresh strawberries and honey.

Nutritional Information:

Calories: 108; Total fat: 20 oz; Total carbohydrates: 32 oz; Protein: 15 oz

Chapter III: Pineapple Salads

Pineapple and Melon Salad with Strawberries

Prep. Time: 15 min. | Servings: 2

Ingredients:

1 can of canned pineapples, cubed

1 cup of small and sweet strawberries, halved

1 small melon, peeled and cubed

1 cup of grapes

3 tablespoons lemon juice, freshly squeezed

1 lemon, chopped

Dressing:

5 tablespoons maple syrup

1 teaspoon pure vanilla extract

½ teaspoon cinnamon

How to Prepare:

1. Combine the cubed pineapple with the halved strawberries, cubed melon, and grapes and mix in the chopped lemon.
2. Now start the dressing by combining the maple syrup, pure vanilla extract, and cinnamon. Don't forget to mix well until there is a smooth consistency. Set aside.
3. Meanwhile, squeeze the lemon to get a fragrant juice.
4. Pour the lemon juice and the sweet salad dressing over the pineapple and melon salad and mix well. Then cover the bowl and place the salad in the fridge for a few hours.

Nutritional Information:

Calories: 89; Total fat: 15 oz; Total carbohydrates: 29 oz; Protein: 9 oz

Pineapple and Melon Salad with Kiwis

Prep. Time: 15 min. | Servings: 2

Ingredients:

1 can of canned pineapples, cubed

2 cups of kiwis, peeled and cubed

1 small melon, peeled and cubed

1 cup of grapes

3 tablespoons lemon juice, freshly squeezed

1 lemon, chopped

Dressing:

5 tablespoons maple syrup

1 teaspoon pure vanilla extract

½ teaspoon cinnamon

How to Prepare:

1. Combine the cubed pineapple with the kiwis, cubed melon, and grapes and mix in the chopped lemon.
2. Now start the dressing by combining the maple syrup, pure vanilla extract, and cinnamon. Don't forget to mix well until there is a smooth consistency. Set aside.

3. Meanwhile, squeeze the lemon to get a fragrant juice.
4. Pour the lemon juice and the sweet salad dressing over the pineapple and melon salad and mix well. Cover the bowl and place the salad in the fridge for a few hours.

<u>Nutritional Information:</u>

Calories: 91; Total fat: 16 oz; Total carbohydrates: 30 oz; Protein: 10 oz

Pineapple and Melon Salad with Pears

Prep. Time: 25 min. | Servings: 4

Ingredients:

1 can of canned pineapples, cubed

4 pears, peeled and cubed

1 small melon, peeled and cubed

1 cup of grapes

3 tablespoons lemon juice, freshly squeezed

1 lemon, chopped

Dressing:

5 tablespoons maple syrup

1 teaspoon pure vanilla extract

½ teaspoon cinnamon

How to Prepare:

1. Combine the cubed pineapple with the pears, cubed melon, and grapes and mix in the chopped lemon.
2. Now start the dressing by combining the maple syrup, pure vanilla extract, and cinnamon. Don't forget to mix well until there is a smooth consistency. Set aside.

3. Meanwhile, squeeze the lemon to get a fragrant juice.
4. Pour the lemon juice and the sweet salad dressing over the pineapple, melon and pears salad and mix well. Cover the bowl and place the salad in the fridge for a few hours. Serve with the spray cream.

Nutritional Information:

Calories: 92; Total fat: 16 oz; Total carbohydrates: 30 oz; Protein: 10 oz

Pineapple Salad with Melon and Apples

Prep. Time: 30 min. | Servings: 2

Ingredients:

1 can of canned pineapple, cubed

2 cups of sour and crispy apples, peeled and cubed

1 melon, peeled and cubed

1 mango, peeled and cubed

2 cups of grapes

5 tablespoons lemon juice, freshly squeezed

Dressing:

5 tablespoons sugar

1 teaspoon pure vanilla extract

½ teaspoon cinnamon

pineapple juice

How to Prepare:

1. Combine the cubed pineapple with the cubed apples, melon, mango and grapes.

2. Now start the dressing by combining the sugar, pure vanilla extract, cinnamon, and pineapple juice. Stir until the sugar dissolves completely and you get the smooth consistency. Taste some mixture using a spoon or a scoop. You shouldn't see or feel any sugar crystals in the spoon, in your mouth or on your tongue. Keep stirring and tasting for few minutes.
3. Meanwhile, squeeze the lemon to get the fresh juice.
4. Pour the lemon juice and the sweet salad dressing over the pineapple salad with melon, mango and apples and mix well. Cover the bowl and place the salad in the fridge for a few hours.

Nutritional Information:

Calories: 89; Total fat: 20 oz; Total carbohydrates: 35 oz; Protein: 10 oz

Pineapple Salad with Melon and Plums

Prep. Time: 25 min. | Servings: 2

Ingredients:

1 can of canned pineapple, cubed

2 cups of plums

1 melon, peeled and cubed

1 mango, peeled and cubed

2 cups of grapes

5 tablespoons lemon juice, freshly squeezed

Dressing:

5 tablespoons sugar

1 teaspoon pure vanilla extract

½ teaspoon cinnamon

pineapple juice

How to Prepare:

1. Combine the cubed pineapple with the plums, melon, mango and grapes.

2. Now start the dressing by combining the sugar, pure vanilla extract, cinnamon, and pineapple juice. Stir until the sugar dissolves completely and you get the smooth consistency. Taste some mixture using a spoon or a scoop. You shouldn't see or feel any sugar crystals in the spoon, in your mouth or on your tongue. Keep stirring and tasting for few minutes.
3. Meanwhile, squeeze the lemon to get the fresh juice.
4. Pour the lemon juice and the sweet salad dressing over the pineapple salad with melon, mango and plums and mix well. Cover the bowl and place the salad in the fridge for a few hours. Serve with the spray cream on top.

Nutritional Information:

Calories: 88; Total fat: 19 oz; Total carbohydrates: 33 oz; Protein: 9 oz

Pineapple Salad with Melon and Hazelnuts

Prep. Time: 25 min. | Servings: 2

Ingredients:

1 can of canned pineapple, cubed

1 cup of hazelnuts

1 melon, peeled and cubed

1 mango, peeled and cubed

2 cups of grapes

5 tablespoons lemon juice, freshly squeezed

Dressing:

5 tablespoons sugar

1 teaspoon pure vanilla extract

½ teaspoon cinnamon

pineapple juice

How to Prepare:

1. Preheat the oven to 250°- 270° Fahrenheit and roast the hazelnuts in the oven for 10 minutes until lightly browned and crispy, then set aside to cool completely. Grind the hazelnuts using a food processor or blender.
2. Combine the cubed pineapple with the hazelnuts, melon, mango and grapes.
3. Now start the dressing by combining the sugar, pure vanilla extract, cinnamon, and pineapple juice. Stir until the sugar dissolves completely and you get the smooth consistency. Taste some mixture using a spoon or a scoop. You shouldn't see or feel any sugar crystals in the spoon, in your mouth or on your tongue. Keep stirring and tasting for few minutes.
4. Meanwhile, squeeze the lemon to get the fresh juice.
5. Pour the lemon juice and the sweet salad dressing over the pineapple, melon, mango and hazelnuts salad and mix well.

Cover the bowl and place the salad in the fridge for a few hours. Serve with the spray cream on top.

Nutritional Information:

Calories: 91; Total fat: 21 oz; Total carbohydrates: 36 oz; Protein: 11 oz

Pineapple, Raspberry and Honey Salad

Prep Time: 24 min. | Servings: 2

Ingredients:

1 big and fresh pineapple, peeled and cubed

2 cups of raspberries

2 mangos, peeled and cubed

2 kiwis, peeled and cubed

5 tablespoons raspberry jam

1 cup of liquid honey

1 teaspoon vanilla

How to Prepare:

1. Combine the raspberry jam with the mangos, kiwis, raspberries and pineapple cubes.
2. After you combine all the pineapple salad ingredients pour the liquid honey over the pineapple and raspberry salad and you are free to serve!

Nutritional Information:

Calories: 114; Total fat: 19 oz; Total carbohydrates: 32 oz; Protein: 14 oz

Pineapple, Strawberry and Honey Salad

Prep Time: 28 min. | Servings: 3

Ingredients:

1 big and fresh pineapple, peeled and cubed

2 cups of strawberries

2 mangos, peeled and cubed

2 kiwis, peeled and cubed

1 cup of strawberry jam

1 cup of liquid honey

1 teaspoon vanilla

spray cream

How to Prepare:

1. Combine the strawberry jam with the mangos, kiwis, strawberries and pineapple cubes.
2. After you combine all the pineapple salad ingredients pour the liquid honey over the pineapple and strawberry salad and you are free to serve with the spray cream on top!

Nutritional Information:

Calories: 101; Total fat: 19 oz; Total carbohydrates: 34 oz; Protein: 14 oz

Pineapple, Blueberry and Honey Salad

Prep Time: 28 min. | Servings: 3

Ingredients:

1 big and fresh pineapple, peeled and cubed

4 cups of blueberries

2 mangos, peeled and cubed

1 cup of oats

2 kiwis, peeled and cubed

1 cup of blueberry jam

1 cup of liquid honey

1 teaspoon vanilla

spray cream

How to Prepare:

1. Combine the blueberry jam with the mangos, kiwis, blueberries and pineapple cubes.
2. Soak the oats in the warm water for 30 minutes.
3. After you combine all the pineapple salad ingredients pour the liquid honey over the pineapple and blueberry salad and you are free to serve with the spray cream on top!

Nutritional Information:

Calories: 102; Total fat: 20 oz; Total carbohydrates: 35 oz; Protein: 15 oz

Pineapple, Oats and Honey Salad

Prep Time: 30 min. | Servings: 2

Ingredients:

1 big and fresh pineapple, peeled and cubed

4 cups of peaches, cubed

2 mangos, peeled and cubed

2 cups of oats

2 kiwis, peeled and cubed

1 cup of peach jam

1 cup of liquid honey

1 teaspoon vanilla

spray cream

How to Prepare:

1. Soak the oats in the warm water for 30 minutes. Combine the peach jam with the mangos, kiwis, peaches and pineapple cubes.
2. After you combine all the pineapple salad ingredients pour the liquid honey over the pineapple and oats salad and you are free to serve the salad with the spray cream on top!

Nutritional Information:

Calories: 103; Total fat: 21 oz; Total carbohydrates: 36 oz; Protein: 16 oz

Pineapple Salad with Pears and Cottage Cheese

Prep Time: 30 min. | Servings: 4

Ingredients:

1 can of canned pineapple chunks, cubed

2 cups of cottage cheese

4 pears, peeled and cubed

1 cup of raisins

4 tablespoons pears jam

Dressing:

4 tablespoons maple syrup

2 tablespoons citric acid

How to Prepare:

1. Soak the raisins in the warm water for 10 minutes.
2. In a bowl, combine the pineapple chunks, raisins, pears, pears jam and cottage cheese.
3. Let's get to the dressing now - beat all the dressing ingredients in a food processor until they have a smooth and creamy consistency.

4. Spoon the dressing over the salad and then mix well.

5. Place the pineapple salad with the pears and cottage cheese in the fridge for 1 hour and then serve with the spray cream on top.

Nutritional Information:

Calories: 120; Total fat: 24 oz; Total carbohydrates: 35 oz; Protein: 14 oz

Pineapple Salad with Peaches and Cottage Cheese

Prep Time: 30 min. | Servings: 4

Ingredients:

1 can of canned pineapple chunks, cubed

2 cups of cottage cheese

4 peaches, pitted and cubed

2 cups of raisins

1 cup of peach jam

Dressing:

4 tablespoons maple syrup

2 tablespoons citric acid

1 teaspoon vanilla

How to Prepare:

1. Soak the raisins in the warm water for 10 minutes.
2. In a bowl, combine the pineapple chunks, raisins, peaches, peach jam and cottage cheese.

3. Let's get to the dressing now - beat all the dressing ingredients in a food processor until they have a smooth and creamy consistency.
4. Pour the dressing over the salad and then mix well.
5. Place the pineapple salad with peaches and cottage cheese in the fridge for 1 hour and then serve with the spray a cream on top.

<u>Nutritional Information:</u>

Calories: 110; Total fat: 21 oz; Total carbohydrates: 33 oz; Protein: 12 oz

Pineapple Salad with Apricots and Cottage Cheese

Prep Time: 30 min. | Servings: 4

Ingredients:

1 can of canned pineapple chunks, cubed

2 cups of cottage cheese

10 apricots, pitted and sliced

1 cup of raisins

5 tablespoons apricot jam

Dressing:

5 tablespoons maple syrup

2 tablespoons citric acid

1 teaspoon vanilla

How to Prepare:

1. Soak the raisins in the warm water for 10 minutes.
2. In a bowl, combine the pineapple chunks, raisins, apricots, apricot jam and cottage cheese.

3. Let's get to the dressing now - beat all the dressing ingredients in a food processor until they have a smooth and creamy consistency.

4. Pour the dressing over the salad and then mix well.

5. Place the pineapple salad with the apricots and cottage cheese in the fridge for 1 hour and then serve with the spray cream on top.

Nutritional Information:

Calories: 119; Total fat: 22 oz; Total carbohydrates: 31 oz; Protein: 13 oz

Pineapple Salad with Bananas and Cottage Cheese

Prep Time: 30 min. | Servings: 4

Ingredients:

1 can of canned pineapple chunks, cubed

2 cups of cottage cheese

4 bananas, peeled and cubed

1 cup of raisins

4 tablespoons banana jam

3 tablespoons cranberries

Dressing:

4 tablespoons maple syrup

2 tablespoons citric acid

1 teaspoon vanilla

How to Prepare:

1. Soak the raisins in the warm water for 10 minutes.
2. In a bowl, combine the pineapple chunks, raisins, bananas, banana jam, cranberries and cottage cheese.
3. Let's get to the dressing now - beat all the dressing ingredients in a food processor until they have a smooth and creamy consistency.
4. Spoon the dressing over the salad and then mix well.
5. Place the pineapple salad with the bananas and cottage cheese in the fridge for 1 hour and then serve with the spray cream on top.

Nutritional Information:

Calories: 125; Total fat: 26 oz; Total carbohydrates: 36 oz; Protein: 15 oz

Pineapple Salad with Strawberries, Cottage Cheese and Cashews

Prep Time: 30 min. | Baking Time: 10 min. | Servings: 4

Ingredients:

1 can of canned pineapple chunks, cubed

2 cups of cottage cheese

4 cups of strawberries

1 cup of raisins

4 tablespoons strawberry jam

2 cups of cashews

Dressing:

4 tablespoons maple syrup

2 tablespoons citric acid

1 teaspoon vanilla

How to Prepare:

1. Preheat the oven to 250°- 270° Fahrenheit and roast the cashews the oven for 10 minutes until lightly browned and

crispy, then set aside to cool completely. Grind the cashews using a food processor or blender.

2. Soak the raisins in the warm water for 10 minutes.
3. In a bowl, combine the pineapple chunks, raisins, strawberries, strawberry jam, cashews and cottage cheese.
4. Let's get to the dressing now - beat all the dressing ingredients in a food processor until they have a smooth and creamy consistency.
5. Spoon the dressing over the salad and then mix well.
6. Place the pineapple salad with the strawberries and cottage cheese in the fridge for 1 hour and then serve with the spray cream on top.

Nutritional Information:

Calories: 135; Total fat: 32 oz; Total carbohydrates: 44 oz; Protein: 19 oz

Pineapple, Oats and Apples Salad

Prep Time: 30 min. | Servings: 2

Ingredients:

1 cup of canned pineapples, cubed

2 cups of sweet apples, peeled and cubed

2 cups of oats

2 mangos, peeled and cubed

1 cup of apple jam

5 tablespoons sugar

1 teaspoon vanilla

4 tablespoons pineapple juice

spray cream

How to Prepare:

1. Soak the oats in the warm water for 10 minutes. Combine the apple jam with the mangos, apples and pineapple cubes.
2. After you combine all the pineapple salad ingredients spoon the sugar over the pineapple and oats salad and you are free to serve the salad with the spray cream on top!

Nutritional Information:

Calories: 105; Total fat: 23 oz; Total carbohydrates: 37 oz; Protein: 17 oz

Pineapple, Oats and Oranges Salad

Prep Time: 35 min. | Servings: 2

Ingredients:

1 cup of canned pineapples, cubed

2 cups of oranges, peeled and cubed

2 cups of oats

2 mangos, peeled and cubed

1 cup of orange jam

5 tablespoons sugar

1 teaspoon vanilla

4 tablespoons pineapple juice

spray cream

How to Prepare:

1. Soak the oats in the warm water for 10 minutes. Combine the orange jam with the mangos, oranges and pineapple cubes.
2. After you combine all the pineapple salad ingredients spoon the sugar and pour the juice over the pineapple and oats salad and you are free to serve the salad with the spray cream on top!

Nutritional Information:

Calories: 105; Total fat: 23 oz; Total carbohydrates: 37 oz; Protein: 17 oz

Pineapple, Oats and Cherry Salad

Prep Time: 35 min. | Servings: 2

Ingredients:

1 cup of canned pineapples, cubed

2 cups of cherries, pitted

2 cups of oats

8 tablespoons cherry jam

5 tablespoons sugar

1 teaspoon vanilla

4 tablespoons pineapple juice

spray cream

How to Prepare:

1. Soak the oats in the warm water for 10 minutes. Combine the cherry jam with the cherries and pineapple cubes.
2. After you combine all the pineapple salad ingredients spoon the sugar and pour the juice over the pineapple and oats salad and you are free to serve the salad with the spray cream on top!

Nutritional Information:

Calories: 107; Total fat: 24 oz; Total carbohydrates: 38 oz; Protein: 18 oz

Spiralized Pineapple Salad with Cranberries and Hazelnuts

Prep Time: 25 min. | Baking Time: 10 min. | Servings: 3

Ingredients:

1 big and fresh pineapple, peeled

1 cup of hazelnuts

1 cup of cranberries

2 pears, peeled and cubed

1 sour apple, peeled and cubed

spray cream

Dressing:

4 tablespoons apple juice

1 teaspoon pure vanilla extract

How to Prepare:

1. Preheat the oven to 270°- 300° Fahrenheit and roast the hazelnuts in the oven for 10 minutes until lightly browned and crispy. Grind the hazelnuts using a food processor.

2. Spiralize or grate the pineapple in Korean style using a Korean carrot grater.
3. Combine the cubed pears with the pineapple, apples, cranberries and hazelnuts.
4. Let's get to the dressing now – combine the apple juice with the pure vanilla extract and beat all ingredients in a blender.
5. Pour the pineapple salad dressing over the salad! Serve this delicious pineapple salad with the spray cream and cold tea.

<u>Nutritional Information:</u>

Calories: 137; Total fat: 21 oz; Total carbohydrates: 28 oz; Protein: 15 oz

Spiralized Pineapple Salad with Peach Jam

Prep Time: 25 min. | Baking Time: 10 min. | Servings: 3

Ingredients:

1 big and fresh pineapple, peeled

2 cups of peach jam

1 cup of hazelnuts

4 peaches, pitted and cubed

1 sour apple, peeled and cubed

spray cream

Dressing:

4 tablespoons pineapple juice

1 teaspoon pure vanilla extract

How to Prepare:

1. Preheat the oven to 270°- 300° Fahrenheit and roast the hazelnuts in the oven for 10 minutes until lightly browned and crispy. Grind the hazelnuts using a food processor.

2. Spiralize or grate the pineapple in Korean style using a Korean carrot grater.
3. Combine the cubed peaches with the pineapple, apple, peach jam and hazelnuts.
4. Let's get to the dressing now – combine the pineapple juice with the pure vanilla extract and beat all ingredients in a blender.
5. Pour the pineapple salad dressing over the salad! Serve this delicious pineapple salad with the spray cream and cold tea.

Nutritional Information:

Calories: 131; Total fat: 22 oz; Total carbohydrates: 29 oz; Protein: 17 oz

Spiralized Pineapple Salad with Strawberry Jam

Prep Time: 25 min. | Baking Time: 10 min. | Servings: 3

Ingredients:

1 big and fresh pineapple, peeled

4 cups of strawberry jam

1 cup of hazelnuts

1 sour apple, peeled and cubed

spray cream

Dressing:

4 tablespoons pineapple juice

1 teaspoon pure vanilla extract

How to Prepare:

1. Preheat the oven to 270°- 300° Fahrenheit and roast the hazelnuts in the oven for 10 minutes until lightly browned and crispy. Grind the hazelnuts using a food processor.
2. Spiralize or grate the pineapple in Korean style using a Korean carrot grater.

3. Combine the cubed apple with the pineapple, strawberry jam and hazelnuts.
4. Let's get to the dressing now – combine the pineapple juice with the pure vanilla extract and beat them in a blender.
5. Pour the pineapple salad dressing over the salad! Serve this delicious pineapple salad with the spray cream and ice cream.

Nutritional Information:

Calories: 132; Total fat: 24 oz; Total carbohydrates: 31 oz; Protein: 18 oz

Pineapple and Blueberries Salad with Mango and Raspberries

Prep Time: 20 min. | Roasting Time: 10 min. | Servings: 4

Ingredients:

1 pineapple, peeled and cubed

2 cups of fresh raspberries

1 cup of fresh strawberries

1 cup of cashews

1 cup of mango, peeled and cubed

5 tablespoons liquid honey

3 teaspoons lemon juice

chocolate cream

How to Prepare:

1. Preheat the oven to 270°- 290° Fahrenheit and roast the cashews in the oven for 10 minutes until lightly browned and crispy, then set aside to cool completely. Grind the cashews.
2. Combine the cubed pineapple with the raspberries, strawberries and roasted cashews.
3. Mix in the mango. Pour the liquid honey and lemon juice over the pineapple and blueberries salad. Then add the chocolate cream on top to serve.

Nutritional Information:

Calories: 125; Total fat: 14 oz; Total carbohydrates: 22 oz; Protein: 12 oz

Pineapple and Blueberries Salad with Kiwis and Raspberries

Prep Time: 20 min. | Roasting Time: 10 min. | Servings: 4

Ingredients:

1 pineapple, peeled and cubed

2 cups of blueberries

2 cups of fresh raspberries

1 cup of fresh strawberries

1 cup of walnuts

1 cup of kiwis, peeled and cubed

5 tablespoons liquid honey

3 teaspoons lemon juice

Chocolate cream

How to Prepare:

1. Preheat the oven to 270°- 290° Fahrenheit and roast the walnuts in the oven for 10 minutes until lightly browned and crispy, then set aside to cool completely. Grind the walnuts.

2. Combine the cubed pineapple with the blueberries, raspberries, strawberries and roasted walnuts.
3. Mix in the cubed kiwis. Pour the liquid honey and lemon juice over the pineapple and blueberries salad. Then add the chocolate cream on top to serve.

Nutritional Information:

Calories: 128; Total fat: 17 oz; Total carbohydrates: 28 oz; Protein: 14 oz

Pineapple Salad with Sour Cream and Berries

Prep Time: 20 min. | Roasting Time: 10 min. | Servings: 4

Ingredients:

1 pineapple, peeled and cubed

2 cup of sour cream

1 cup of fresh raspberries

1 cup of fresh strawberries

1 cup of cashews

1 cup of mango, peeled and cubed

1 cup of white sugar

chocolate cream

How to Prepare:

1. Preheat the oven to 270°- 290° Fahrenheit and roast the cashews in the oven for 10 minutes until lightly browned and crispy, then set aside to cool completely. Grind the cashews.
2. Beat the sour cream with the sugar using an electric hand mixer until the creamy consistency and homogenous mass.

3. Combine the cubed pineapple with the raspberries, strawberries and roasted cashews.
4. Mix in the mango. Pour the sour cream over the pineapple and berries salad. Then add the chocolate cream on top to serve.

Nutritional Information:

Calories: 145; Total fat: 23 oz; Total carbohydrates: 33 oz; Protein: 18 oz

Pineapple Salad with Sour Cream and Kiwis

Prep Time: 20 min. | Roasting Time: 10 min. | Servings: 4

Ingredients:

1 pineapple, peeled and cubed

2 cup of sour cream

2 cups of kiwis

1 cup of fresh strawberries

1 cup of hazelnuts

1 cup of pears, peeled and cubed

1 cup of white sugar

chocolate cream

How to Prepare:

1. Preheat the oven to 270°- 290° Fahrenheit and roast the hazelnuts in the oven for 10 minutes until lightly browned and crispy, then set aside to cool completely. Grind the hazelnuts.
2. Beat the sour cream with the sugar using an electric hand mixer until the creamy consistency and homogenous mass.
3. Combine the cubed pineapple with the kiwis, strawberries and roasted hazelnuts.
4. Mix in the pears. Pour the sour cream over the pineapple and kiwis salad. Then add the chocolate cream on top to serve.

Nutritional Information:

Calories: 147; Total fat: 25 oz; Total carbohydrates: 35 oz; Protein: 19 oz

Pineapple Salad with Sour Cream and Bananas

Prep Time: 25 min. | Roasting Time: 10 min. | Servings: 2

Ingredients:

1 pineapple, peeled and cubed

2 cup of sour cream

5 bananas, peeled and cubed

1 cup of fresh strawberries

1 cup of cashews

1 cup of pears, peeled and cubed

1 cup of white sugar

Chocolate cream

How to Prepare:

1. Preheat the oven to 270°- 290° Fahrenheit and roast the cashews in the oven for 10 minutes until lightly browned and crispy, then set aside to cool completely. Grind the cashews.
2. Beat the sour cream with the sugar using an electric hand mixer until the creamy consistency and homogenous mass.

3. Combine the cubed pineapple with the bananas, strawberries and roasted cashews.
4. Mix in the pears and pour the sour cream over the pineapple and bananas salad ingredients. Then add the chocolate cream on top to serve.

<u>Nutritional Information:</u>

Calories: 145; Total fat: 24 oz; Total carbohydrates: 34 oz; Protein: 20 oz

Chapter IV: Pineapple Pies

Pineapple Pie with Strawberries

Prep Time: 30 min. | Baking Time: 40 min. | Servings: 5

Ingredients:

9" or 11" in diameter pie crust (pastry shell)

1 big and fresh pineapple, peeled and grated

2 cups of strawberries

1 cup of toffee bits, chopped

4 cups of white sugar

1 cup of strawberry jam

1 teaspoon cinnamon

½ teaspoon cloves, ground

1 cup unsalted butter

How to Prepare:

1. Spoon the sugar over the strawberries and mash them using the potato masher. Mash the strawberries with the sugar until there is a smooth consistency. Set the strawberries aside.
2. In a saucepan, melt the butter. Mix in the pineapples, strawberries, cinnamon and cloves and stew for around 20 minutes over low heat with the closed lid until there is a smooth consistency. Add in the strawberry jam.
3. Spoon the pineapple mixture into the pastry shell and add one cup of the toffees on top, and then bake for 40 minutes.
4. 10 minutes before the pineapple pie with strawberries is ready open the oven and spoon one cup of toffee bits on top. Serve with the spray cream and coffee.

Nutritional Information:

Calories: 154; Total fat: 25 oz; Total carbohydrates: 36 oz; Protein: 17 oz

Pineapple Pie with Raspberries

Prep Time: 30 min. | Baking Time: 40 min. | Servings: 5

Ingredients:

9" or 11" in diameter pie crust (pastry shell)

1 big and fresh pineapple, peeled and grated

2 cups of raspberries

1 cup of toffee bits, chopped

4 cups of white sugar

1 cup of raspberry jam

1 teaspoon cinnamon

½ teaspoon cloves, ground

1 cup unsalted butter

How to Prepare:

1. Spoon the sugar over the raspberries and mash them using the potato masher. Mash the raspberries with the sugar until there is a smooth consistency. Set the raspberries aside.
2. In a saucepan, melt the butter. Mix in the pineapples, raspberries, cinnamon and cloves and stew for around 20 minutes over low heat with the closed lid until there is a smooth consistency. Add in the raspberry jam.

3. Spoon the pineapple mixture into the pastry shell and add one cup of the toffees on top, and then bake for 40 minutes.
4. 10 minutes before the pineapple pie with raspberries is ready open the oven and spoon one cup of toffee bits on top. Serve with the spray cream and coffee.

Nutritional Information:

Calories: 155; Total fat: 26 oz; Total carbohydrates: 37 oz; Protein: 19 oz

Pineapple Pie with Blueberries

Prep Time: 30 min. | Baking Time: 40 min. | Servings: 5

Ingredients:

9" or 11" in diameter pie crust (pastry shell)

1 big and fresh pineapple, peeled and grated

2 cups of blueberries

1 cup of toffee bits, chopped

4 cups of white sugar

1 cup of blueberry jam

1 teaspoon cinnamon

½ teaspoon cloves, ground

1 cup unsalted butter

How to Prepare:

1. Spoon the sugar over the blueberries and mash them using the potato masher. Mash the blueberries with the sugar until there is a smooth consistency. Set the blueberries aside.
2. In a saucepan, melt the butter. Mix in the pineapples, blueberries, cinnamon and cloves and stew for around 20 minutes over low heat with the closed lid until there is a smooth consistency. Add in the blueberry jam.
3. Spoon the pineapple mixture into the pastry shell and add one cup of the toffees on top, and then bake for 40 minutes.
4. 10 minutes before the pineapple pie with the blueberries is ready open the oven and spoon one cup of toffee bits on top. Serve with the spray cream and coffee.

Nutritional Information:

Calories: 156; Total fat: 26 oz; Total carbohydrates: 38 oz; Protein: 19 oz

Pineapple Pie with Gooseberries

Prep Time: 30 min. | Baking Time: 40 min. | Servings: 5

Ingredients:

9" or 11" in diameter pie crust (pastry shell)

1 big and fresh pineapple, peeled and grated

2 cups of gooseberries

1 cup of toffee bits, chopped

4 cups of white sugar

1 cup of gooseberry jam

1 teaspoon cinnamon

½ teaspoon cloves, ground

1 cup unsalted butter

How to Prepare:

1. Spoon the sugar over the gooseberries and mash them using the potato masher. Mash the gooseberries with the sugar until there is a smooth consistency.

2. In a saucepan, melt the butter. Mix in the pineapples, gooseberries, cinnamon and cloves and stew for around 20 minutes over low heat with the closed lid until there is a smooth consistency. Add in the gooseberry jam.

3. Spoon the pineapple mixture into the pastry shell and add one cup of the toffees on top, and then bake for 40 minutes.
4. 10 minutes before the pineapple pie with gooseberries is ready open the oven and spoon one cup of toffee bits on top. Serve with the spray cream and coffee.

Nutritional Information:

Calories: 156; Total fat: 27 oz; Total carbohydrates: 38 oz; Protein: 20 oz

Pineapple Pie with Apples, Cinnamon and Hazelnuts

Prep Time: 25 min. | Baking Time: 50 min. | Servings: 3

Ingredients:

9" or 11" in diameter pie crust (pastry shell)

1 fresh pineapple, peeled and grated

4 sour apples, peeled and grated

1 teaspoon cinnamon

2 cups of hazelnuts

3 cups of white sugar

½ teaspoon cloves, ground

1 cup of unsalted butter

How to Prepare:

1. In a skillet, melt the unsalted butter.
2. Preheat the oven and roast the hazelnuts in the oven for 5-10 minutes until lightly browned and crispy, then set aside to cool completely. Grind the hazelnuts using a food processor or blender.
3. In a saucepan, combine the pineapples, apples, sugar, butter, cinnamon and cloves and stew for around 20 minutes over low heat with the closed lid until there is a smooth consistency. Then mix in the hazelnuts.
4. Spoon the pineapple, chocolate and walnuts mixture into the pastry shell and add one cup of the toffees on top, and then bake for around 45-50 minutes.
5. 10 minutes before the pineapple and walnuts pie is ready open the oven and spoon one cup of toffee bits on top. Serve with the spray cream and milk.

Nutritional Information:

Calories: 167; Total fat: 26 oz; Total carbohydrates: 44 oz; Protein: 21 oz

Pineapple Pie with Cottage Cheese

Prep Time: 15 min. | Baking Time: 1 h | Servings: 6

Ingredients:

2 cups of wheat flour

2 teaspoons baking powder

1 teaspoon vanilla

2 cups of unsalted butter

1 teaspoon baking spray

Filling:

2 medium pineapples, peeled and grated

2 cups of cottage cheese

1 cup of wheat flour

2 cups of sugar

2 teaspoons cinnamon

1 cup of cream

half cup cashews

How to Prepare:

1. Preheat the oven to 250°-270° Fahrenheit and roast the cashews in the oven until golden brown and crispy, then coat the pie pan with the baking spray or butter and leave it in the oven to melt the butter.
2. In a big bowl, combine the pineapples with 1 cup of the sugar and leave for 15 minutes.
3. In a second bowl, combine the flour, baking powder, butter and vanilla and mix well.
4. Blend the mixture with the water until the dough has a smooth consistency and then pin out the dough and place it into the pie pan.
5. Prepare the pie filling now – combine the flour with the sugar, cinnamon, 1/3 of pineapples, cottage cheese and cashews.
6. Spoon 1/3 of the pineapples on the crust and then spoon half of the flour mixture on top. Top with the grated pineapples

and second part of the flour mixture. Pour the cream and place the butter slices on top.

7. Place the pineapple pie into the oven and bake for 1 hour until the top of the pie is golden brown and crispy.

Nutritional Information:

Calories: 285; Total fat: 38 oz; Total carbohydrates: 52 oz; Protein: 29 oz

Pineapple Pie with Apples and Honey

Prep Time: 15 min. | Baking Time: 1 hour | Servings: 4

Ingredients:

9" or 11" in diameter pie crust (pastry shell)

1 big and fresh pineapple, peeled and cubed

4 apples, peeled and cubed

1 cup of honey

1 cup of walnuts

2 cups of sugar

1 teaspoon cinnamon

½ teaspoon cloves, ground

1 cup of unsalted butter

How to Prepare:

1. In a skillet, melt the unsalted butter for around 5-10 minutes.
2. Preheat the oven to 250°- 270° Fahrenheit and roast the walnuts in the oven for 10 minutes until lightly browned and crispy, then set aside to cool completely. Grind the walnuts using a food processor or blender.
3. In a saucepan, combine the pineapples, apples, sugar, butter, cinnamon and cloves, and stew for around 20 minutes over low heat with the closed lid. Mix in the walnuts and honey.
4. Spoon the pineapple and apples mixture into the pastry shell and bake for around 40 minutes.
5. Serve the pineapple pie with apples and honey with the spray cream and hot milk.

Nutritional Information:

Calories: 159; Total fat: 24 oz; Total carbohydrates: 37 oz; Protein: 17 oz

Conclusion

Thank you for buying this fourth pineapple recipe book. I hope this cookbook was able to help you prepare delicious pineapple recipes, such as pies, salads or hot dishes.

If you've enjoyed this book, I'd greatly appreciate if you could leave your honest opinion.

Your direct feedback could be used to help other readers to discover the advantages of pineapple recipes!

Thank you again and I hope you have enjoyed this pineapple cookbook.

Recipe Index

Apples (54, 78, 108, 113) Apricots (72) Bananas (36, 74, 98) Beef (22, 26) Beer (18) Blueberries (46, 90, 92, 104) Cabbage (28) Cashews (76) Cherries (42) Chicken (8, 10, 12) Cinnamon (108) Coconut (42, 44, 46) Cottage cheese (68, 70, 72, 74, 76, 110) Cranberries (84) Eggplant (8) Gooseberries (106) Hazelnuts (58, 84, 108) Honey (61, 62, 64, 66, 113) Kiwi (50, 92, 96) Mango (90) Melon (48, 50, 52, 54, 56, 58) Oats (66, 78, 80, 82) Oranges (80) Onions (26) Peaches (38, 70) Peanuts (36, 38, 40) Pears (52, 68) Plums (56) Pork (14, 16, 18, 20) Pumpkin (14, 16, 32) Raspberry (61) Squash (10, 30) Sour Cream (94, 96, 98) Strawberries (40, 44, 48, 76, 100) Sweetcorns (12) Wine (16)